BLACK SHAWL

BLACK SHAWL

p o e m s

Kathryn Stripling Byer

LOUISIANA STATE UNIVERSITY PRESS

Baton Rouge

1998

Copyright © 1983, 1988, 1989, 1990, 1992, 1993, 1995, 1996, 1997, 1998 by Kathryn Stripling Byer
All rights reserved
Manufactured in the United States of America
First printing
07 06 05 04 03 02 01 00 99 98   5 4 3 2 1

Designer: Amanda McDonald Key
Typeface: Granjon
Typesetter: Wilsted & Taylor Publishing Services
Printer and binder: Thomson–Shore, Inc.

Library of Congress Cataloging-in-Publication Data
Byer, Kathryn Stripling.
    Black shawl : poems / Kathryn Stripling Byer.
    p.   cm.
    ISBN 0-8071-2250-5 (cloth : alk. paper). — ISBN 0-8071-2251-3
(pbk. : alk. paper)
    I. Title.
PS3569.T6965B94   1998
811'.54—dc21   97-46082
                                                CIP

Grateful acknowledgment is made to the editors of the following publications, in which the poems noted first appeared: *Asheville Poetry Review:* "Timberline," "Wa'ya"; *Asheville Review:* "Síle"; *Emrys* (Women in the Arts issue): "She"; *English Journal:* "Full Moon," "Delphia"; *Georgia Journal:* "Dulcimer," "When the Wind"; *Georgia Review:* "Circuit Rider," "Mountain Time," "Night Shade," "Rose of Sharon"; *Greensboro Review:* "Before Dawn," "The Lookout," "The Morning of the First Day"; *North Carolina Humanities Review:* "Ripe"; *North Carolina Literary Review:* "Blood Mountain," "Backwater"; *Shenandoah:* "Wild," "Snow Breath," "Tobacco"; *The Siren:* "New Hat"; *Southern Review:* "The Devil's Dream."

"Tuckasegee" first appeared in *Alma* (Phoenix Hill Press, 1983). "Sisters" first appeared, in a somewhat different form, as "Indigo" in *Wildwood Flower* (LSU Press, 1992).

"Mountain Time" is for Joyce Moore, for whose bookstore's grand opening I originally wrote this poem. "Blood Mountain" is for Fred Chappell. "Backwater" is for Moira Bailis, who kindly sent me several translations of "Caillech Bérri," as well as other information on early Irish poetry.

My thanks to James Applewhite, Isabel Zuber, and my husband, Jim Byer, for their help in the preparation of this manuscript. And my gratitude to Willa Mae Pressley, whose memories of her mother, Delphia Potts, were the source for several of these poems.

The paper in this book meets the guidelines for permanence and durability of the Committee on Production Guidelines for Book Longevity of the Council on Library Resources. ♾

For Lee Smith
and
in memory of
Sharon Anglin Kuhne and Edward Krickel

C O N T E N T S

News travels slowly up here
in the mountains, our narrow
roads twisting for days, maybe years,
till we get where we're going,
if we ever do. Even if some lonesome message
should make it through Deep Gap
or the fastness of Thunderhead, we're not obliged
to believe it's true, are we? Consider
the famous poet, minding her post
at the Library of Congress, who
shrugged off the question of what we'd be
reading at century's end: "By the year 2000
nobody will be reading poems." Thus she
prophesied. End of that
interview! End of the world
as we know it. Yet, how can I fault
her despair, doing time as she was
in a crumbling Capitol, sirens
and gunfire the nights long, the Pentagon's
stockpile of weapons stacked higher
and higher? No wonder the books
stacked around her began to seem relics.
No wonder she dreamed her own bones
dug up years later, tagged in a museum somewhere
in the Midwest: American Poet—Extinct Species.

Up here in the mountains
we know what extinct means. We've seen
how our breath on a bitter night
fades like a ghost from the window glass.
We know the wolf's gone.
The panther. We've heard the old stories

run down, stutter out
into silence. Who knows where we're heading?
All roads seem to lead
to Millennium, dark roads with drop-offs
we can't plumb. It's time to be brought up short
now with the tale-teller's *Listen:* There once lived
a woman named Delphia
who walked through these hills teaching children
to read. She was known as a quilter
whose hand never wearied, a mother
who raised up two daughters to pass on
her words like a strong chain of stitches.
Imagine her sitting among us,
her quick thimble moving along these lines
as if to hear every word striking true
as the stab of her needle through calico.
While prophets discourse about endings,
don't you think she'd tell us the world as we know it
keeps calling us back to beginnings?
This labor to make our words matter
is what any good quilter teaches.
A stitch in time, let's say.
A blind stitch
that clings to the edges
of what's left, the ripped
scraps and remnants, whatever
won't stop taking shape even though the whole
crazy quilt's falling to pieces.

. . . Nights I can't
sleep I hear
wind shove the dead
leaves along like my own
thoughts, those rag
taggle gypsies she sang
about, all of them black
shawled and stealing
away to their dirty
work. . . .
　　　　"What
will you make
of this?" they whisper,
filling my arms
with a snatch of her
hair, muddy ribbons, this
tangle of black roots
that drags my hands down.

—"Black Shawl"
　from *Wildwood Flower*

They had no use
for such romance as clings
like the stubbornest

ivy. Those gypsy-black boots
in the stirrups,
those gay golden rings left

behind on a pillow, what good
to them, nursing their babies
and watching the gangplanks beginning

to rise on the ships named Prosperity,
Rainbow, Glorious
Memory? *Having no say*

in their journey, they came
here. They stood
on the high ridges, listening

into the ceaseless
wind sounding the bedrock
of what lay beyond them.

At nightfall they pulled shut
the doors of their cabins
and blew out their lanterns.

They waited.
What else could they do?
But when they sang

their solitude into
those old songs of love
and betrayal, each verse

must have called like a path
to them, braving the laurel
hells, rockslides

and bottomless chasms.
How else journey
into those distances

where they heard night
after night in the new world
the dark itself howl

like a woman cast into
the wilderness? One by
one, I see them open their mouths.

Here I am,
they sing,
having become their own voices.

Caught in my basin, the moon
shimmies. She must feel low
down tonight, floating there
like some big-city show

girl's silk underwear,
daring me stir up her lather
and scrub till I'm crazy
with moonshine, the better

to see my way clear
through the thick of my mama's
keep, thirsty for what makes
my teeth ache. This summer

I've nothing to dream on but dirt
roads, my mouth full
of singing that swells like the creek
jumping bank at the pull

of the honky-tonk season.
I'm game to go prowling
the backwoods with every bitch
loosed for a dozen miles, howling

at first sight of her rising
over the pine scrub of Hell's
Thicket, where in the last
eyes of wolf I hear tell

of, she still
burns, closing in for the kill.

No, I'll not listen.
The sound of it's too sweet,
like honey I licked from the spoon
while he sat on my porch
and played *Shady Grove.*
"You are the darling of my heart,
stay till the sun goes down."

I remember the hoot owl came closer.
Moths burned their wings in his candle wick.
"Midnight," I said,
and his fingers stirred wind from the strings,
begging, Stay, while he cradled the wood in his lap
for a last song, the hazel-

green eyes of a lost lady.
Weep Willow.
Soul of the laurel shade.
"Come," he said, pointing through dark

to the bed of leaves
we'd gathered, wildflowers strewn
on a pillow of moss.

But I sent him away,
letting go of his hand
without whispering as I do
now when my wits fail me, *oh my*
sweet, nothing
but sweet
good for nothing man.

Handsome man, come with your black book to judge
me, I'll not ask you down for so much as a sip
from my bucketful. Stay in your saddle
and preach God's arrival. I'll listen.

I'll listen to anything. Left to my porch
I can see, past the stave of your hat brim,
the silverbell blooming its faraway music. Yes,
I know my price. Beyond rubies and diamonds.

Soul? Oh, that flimsy of silk hand-me-down,
it does not want to snuggle in Abraham's
bosom! It wants a strong wind. Let it fly
with the smallest of God's many sparrows.

This body you say will decay desires nothing
but sally grass, sycamore shade. Where my grave
waits is nobody's business. I walk on it
when I go trailing the first scent of dog hobble

into the dark that's already begun creeping
down from the laurel hells where I hear something
wild holding out, maybe the last wolf alive
on this mountain. He's hungry. Before long

we'll both hear him howling. Don't shout!
I believe every hair on my head has been numbered.
Lean closer. I'll untie my kerchief
and you can let God help you count them.

Fancy, you called
it, your fiddling that filled
up the green hollow
come the first warm
nights, but what has this song
got to do with me
now, this bedevilment
whispering all the way home
along Beggarman's Trace
like the rustle of silken
hems over the muddy
ruts? Roots of the black
walnut tree are what
I want this morning,
the bark of the spruce pine
and chestnut oak. I'll weave
a grave sheet that hangs
silent. Night
cloak that nevermore
roams. Something final
now I am as nothing
to you but some chaff
blown away on
the slightest breeze. Shifting
sand. Dust unto
dust. What's the Devil's own
dream but to be
snagged forever on
April, like me among
blackberry briars, letting wind
in these leaves tease
my fancy? *He wants me,*
He wants me not. I know
what you want. To wade into
deep water with me,
your hand on my head

meant to save me from
hearing again how
the hatchling frogs down
by the river sing
some other god's resurrection.

Its ribbons knot under my chin
like the goiter my grandmother
hid under lace collars
when there was company. Two apples.

Scarlet plume. Green
bird of paradise. Where will I wear
such a monstrous reminder of me
in the mayflowers that spring the flood

came? I saw the road brimming
with sky like a message
I read wrong. "To high ground,"
he called, and I followed,

my gingham skirt hitched above briars.
We sat with our meal sack of cornbread,
our jug of cold buttermilk, waving the world
on its way, kitchen tables

and tin cans, what looked like
a bonnet the brown water waltzed
while I laughed, as if
there were no woman left homeless upriver.

blows
a bell rings, but
barely. The sickle
moon's ghost
ear floats over
us, listening,
listening. Branches
creak, idle swings
clatter, a bucket's
blown clear
across somebody's
backyard. You whistle
the same song as last
night: a cold
cold heart that wants
melting. We sat
up late, wine
glowing. *Winefire*
I whispered,
as if it were nothing
but spirits had
brought us to Burning
Wing Gap where the golden
leaves lay down
a carpet we climbed
till the sky stopped
us. You took my fingers
and rubbed them
like flint. Kindled
fear: scent of late
summer wildfire,
the loud bell,
and all night the silence
of fields having given
themselves up
to burning.

Snow on the mountains.
Where did the wind go? I stand with my shawl
wrapped around me and listen.

Snow on the mountains.
The holly-pip red as a blood blister,
thorns reaching out to me.

Snow on the mountains.
Don't beg me to come back inside
lest I catch my death.

Snow on the mountains.
The river a hard road to travel.
My feet slide on ice cobble.

Snow on the mountains.
Gone south, I will say when you shout
from the riverbank.

Snow on the mountains.
Against my ear you held a conch shell once,
asking *What do you hear?*

So much snow on the mountains,
I hitched up my dress and ran home.
How could I tell you then,

hearing snow on the mountains
refuse to melt, that after so long,
a woman's soul searching

through snow on the mountains
will sink, out of breath, in the silence
of nothing more, nothing less.

I never
dared climb

to the edge
of its scarp

till I ripped
my gown running

the straight-up trail
after him

though he was
already half the night

gone. There I stood
looking deep

into nowhere
as if I might see

how to go on
without going back

down the trail
to his house where

I'd have to take
twice-doubled thread

to my tatters, the way
flesh itself heals,

the white scar-stitch
mending the rutted

hide. How many
times have I seen since

that morning
what up here the distance

makes clear? East
to west can't be joined

but by countless miles
hard traveling unto the ends

of the earth. Tell me,
where is the thread

knotted strong enough?
How shut the needle's eye

through which
a woman might stare

all her life down
and down,

taking no
for an answer?

Grandmama chewed
mouthfuls ripe as
wild plums. Spat. Missed
houseflies and hound

dogs that stirred up
the dust. Her front
porch mottled brown.
Honey, idle

that cuspidor
closer, can't see
where I'm aiming.
I pushed the can

close with a stick.
Ran. She don't miss
a trick, said her
old man who hid

in the shed with
his whiskey. She
sees better, hears
better, what's more

she'll live longer'n
you or me. Don't
ever ask her
for anything,

Mama said. She
won't say doodley-
squat. Just let her
sit. Chew her cud.

Cow. The devil
take her black tongue.

I lie in bed, knowing the first cold spell's
wakened me early. I dread to see beans

climbing nowhere, their blackened shells
strung along vines that wind chain

upon chain round the straw corn. Should any nest,
blown from the sky with a jot

of blue stuck to its innermost
thatching, land next to my bare foot,

I'd kick it away! Would I risk my own
child finding strands of her gold hair

tight-woven with beasts' fur and barn
wattle? Not yet. I've learned to keep doors

shut. Why shiver? I know well
enough what's to see past the fringe

of my lilacs—the waiting hill
littered with red plastic flowers I'd cringe

to be offered. Let sleeping bones lie
till the dawn when my husband's kin

rise from the rubble. On Sundays his people stop by
for a last look, then turn to my table their thin

lips that mumble may God's will be done. *What
a pity,* his mother says, meaning the stone

bed of some distant cousin's brat.
Come cold, how many more small ones?

Even before she was born, I would hold
her too hard against Raven's Deep flooding,
while I fought to stand in that nightmare
releasing me always the moment I lost

her, the rush of her face screaming *Mama*
swept from me so fast I would throw back
the sheet, thinking I heard her voice
calling. Not calling. Always the thunder

of whitewater down the falls, ceaseless
as rain seemed to hammer our tin roof
that April she wandered too far and I had to risk
mudslide and creeks rearing out of their beds

till I found her asleep in the thick
of a laurel shade. Nothing could wake her
while she slept what I knew too well was the sleep
of the drowned. Neither hailstone

nor cloudburst. Nor close by, the cry
of a panther. The gunshots that silenced it.
Surely not my witless fear prowling
into her room every night where she lay

quiet. Too quiet. What was she hiding
from me while the cold lap of moonlight around
my bare feet ebbed and flowed and I swayed
like a willow branch over her slumber?

I cross my hands on my breast
and tell my heart be done beating
Rose Red,
Rose White,
as my mother said
she would have named us,
myself being Rose Red because
of my blooming face
held up to her after Rose White
had died in the granny's arms,
so soon turned blue
as a spindle of indigo let fall
at noontime. Oh hurry,
please put her back into the dark
ground, my mother says
she cried, so they dug my sister's grave
forthwith and buried her
wrapped in the only white tablecloth
Mama had left at our birthing,
her other nine buds gone
to dirt in the tangledy garden
she won't let me walk through
for fear of snakes coiled
beneath tall weeds, the offspring
of Satan himself.
I must keep within sight,
lest I blossom too soon
and my petals blow into the wilderness
where for a little while we must camp,
Mama sings, asking ourselves are
we ready, oh ready. Each night ever closer
its weeds crawl, its vines climbing over
our roof. Gusts of birds
every daybreak beat louder.
Their beaks at my window glass
tap. Who will save me,
I wonder, as I pleat these white tissue

roses I gather for garlands
and bridal bouquets. (Now the nick
of a hatpin! Some blood
from my finger squeezed into each
center.) Whoever he is,
when he comes with his silver
axe swinging, his saw-teeth
that grin through the laurel
hells, I will be Rose
Among Wild Roses. I will be Rose
Willing. I will be ready.

Full moon says look I am
over the pinebreak, says give me
your empty glass, pour
all you want, drink, look
out through your windows of ice,
through the eyes of your needles
observe how I climb, lay aside
what you weave on your looms

and see clouds fall away
like cold silk from your shoulders,
be quiet, hear the owl coming back
to the hayloft, shake loose
your long braids and rise up
from your beds, open
windows and curtains, let light
pour like water upon your heads,

all of you women who wait, raise
the shades, throw the shutters
wide, lean from your window ledge
into the great night that beckons
you, smile back at me
and so quietly nobody can hear you
but you, whisper, "Here am I."

Part 2

BLOOD MOUNTAIN

Legend says Creek
battled Cherokee
down to the last
man and left
these rocks stained
with their warriors' blood,

but if you ask
the old woman threading
her loom on the outskirts
of town how this
place got its name,
she says one story's
good as another
so long as there's
blood in it.

of their bone she was. Blood-tied
the whole length of Beggarman's Trace.
Was there nobody she was not kin to?
She dared not walk out of a night by herself

and by day she stayed close to the house
or else scuttled through low-lying snags
like a creature her cousins' dogs hunted.
She learned how to fight her way

free when she could. When she could
not, to play dead. To let them make always
the same boast: *That little gal's not going anywhere.*
What good to run away into some dark night

where every lamp signified kinsmen?
And kinswomen who would not look up, not once,
from the snarls in their warp chains, or carding wool
bunched in their laps, to say anything?

At the loom she sat braiding
her sister's hair. Hitching it tight
with a warping string. "There,

she said. "There!" And turned back
to her silent walk. Kitchen to bedroom to washbasin,
grinding her fist into palm

like a spade against rock
until wind sweeping fast down the ridge
made the house tremble. "Go pull the shutters,

you hear me? Don't dawdle," she yelled,
startled out of her pantomime,
not angry now but afraid of the thundercloud

swelling on Buzzard's Roost,
black as the bruises he'd left on her arms
when he found her too far down the footpath

and drove her back home wiping blood
from her mouth with the hem
of her calicoes. "Christ, it's a wild one!"

she cried as the storm tumbled hail
on his cornfield. Her hand at the dead bolt
shook. "Stay close,"

she whispered, afraid if she opened
the door, she'd have no other choice but to go
where the wind took her

even as lightning snaked down
like the whip he made dance
round her running feet when he got drunk

and she wanted to scream
at him, "Go ahead,
strike me. I dare you!"

Gently, as if swabbing
wounds, she scrubs
stains left from

where they lay down
in the grass. She remembers
her fingers plunged deep

into crushed green, the odor
of light rain, the moldering
leaves going up in a fever

of white flowers till she
can hear herself babbling
such words as *forever,*

*forget-me-not, full
moon,* her mouth
like a dovecote of syllables

forced open so she can
taste every sweet
nothing melting away

into silence as she lay
beneath him like trampled
earth already trying

to cover itself with a veil
of such snowy white
as what a bride calls (oh

why can't she hear
what she says?) *Sheer
Illusion.*

The last thing she did
before she disappeared was cut
warp threads and leave them
to gather the handful

of blue yarn scraps
next morning. Then she was
over and done with.
Not even a note

though they looked on the floor.
In the grass. Called her name
down the trace. She had taken
some two-day-old cornbread

and left the back door
open. They were too young
to doubt she had been stolen
away into that gypsy

ballad she must have been
singing, her last
weaving flung like a lie
round her shoulders.

Tonight by the flare
of a pine knot, his stallion tears
clean through the limp fog that lays
itself down along Beggarman's Trace.

When he stops at the Jump-Off
to guzzle more whiskey, she coughs
at his back till he turns, and his breath
in her face smells like death

or close to it. Below, lamps illumine
the houses where she should know women
are already telling how she's become nothing
but wind they hear mouthing

temptation: *Let Go.* (Now she's
no longer neighbor, they'll let her be
damned to a shallow grave.) They try
to listen as far as they can for the cry

of the bobcat their men will be out
tracking all night. They want it brought
down by its throat or else, goodness knows,
what's running wild might come too close.

Maple leaves pool
in a gully
where could be she

slept. Or kept watch
while he scouted
the darkness, his gun

at the ready,
his knife strung alongside
his left thigh.

How long did they search
for her this time,
her name thrown the length

of the sheer traces, ropes
over ledges to thorny
beds, dragging the deep

river bottoms? Now ash
berries swell to a bouquet
she'd understand,

hunted downwind
as she was by the balladeers
hot on the scent

of a good story
everyone knows
ends with blood.

And if anyone asks
who she really was,
let's say a woman

who made her escape
from this mountain come dawn.
Or else didn't.

she didn't.
Let's say he left her behind
not at all dead
but calmly addressing a wrenched ankle,
muttering what she remembered of some silly
granny-chant: *Hucklebone, hucklebone.*
Let's say she hobbled back home
and proceeded to live out her days
either waiting for blood
or else scrubbing its tracks
from her bedsheets and shifts,
not to mention the manifold bandages
torn from old petticoats.
Soaked every month in a boiling pot,
they bubbled thinner and thinner
till nothing was left
but her blood in the water
she stirred to a rising tide.
Nights she could hear it,
the same as had washed from her body at childbirth
and now welled and oozed from the cut thumbs
and first-cloven lips of her children.
The same as what puddled
the floor when she gutted wild game
on her chopping block, what brimmed
her hands when she raided the hanging pig's
ripped belly, what dripped
and dripped from the pig's snout. The pails
she could fill with it!
Old blood and first
blood and bad blood and cold blood and blue
blood and blood in her mouth
from a bit tongue
whenever she heard round
the quilt circle tales of another girl
gone down the mountain in the dead
of night, leaving
no more than a fiction
of snapped twigs to follow.

Part 3

DELPHIA

Dead end.
This dirt road
at daybreak.

One window
burns yellow
as fruit flesh.

The gauze
clutch of spider webs
almost

but not quite
shines. Where is the sun?
Where the woman who lately leaned

over her washbasin,
daring the cold water
splash her eyes shut?

She does
not answer
anyone's name.

Have her feet
come unstuck
from the kitchen floor

where she stood
most of last
night at her stove

spinning
wild berry
juice into

length
upon length of the sweetest
black thread?

told them the truth early on
when they started to play round her quilting frame
holding what she had decreed would be
Cullowhee Valley's most bountiful rose garden.
What keeps the whole blooming
patchwork from falling to pieces
is stitches no bigger than pinpricks,
she told them, so fasten your calicoes steady by mites
and they'll hold till the last of you
lies dreaming under these pretty scraps.
Don't let light waning just before
suppertime hurry you into a tangle
you'll have to pick out with your fingernails.
Ever pick cornsilk from out of the shucked
nubs, you'll know what I mean.
Just remember the light will come back
for another day's labor. You'll wake
to see pine needles pressed
against window glass, glory vines cascading
this way and that, and you'll know what you want
is a pattern that makes of this world
more than Fleur-de-Lis, Goose Wing,
and Waterwheel bounded by what I remember
a neighbor called Worm Border
though I myself prefer Snail
Creep or Dog Trail.
Don't ask me the big questions
none but a fool tries to answer
straight. All I can tell you of why
you were born is to take your own time
once the needle's been threaded,
the stray thimble fetched from the cloth bag.
Come closer
and I'll swing the gate to my ring-around Rose Garden.
I'll show you Cross and Crown.
Bluebirds.
I'll show you the Rainbow,

Stepping Stones, Dove in the Window,
the Winding Way.
What are you waiting for?

> *Sit down.*
> *Sit down.*

Over me, wind
rattled every loose board
while she gathered me into her black shawl
that smelled of the smoky hearth.
Summer's gone, she said,

and parting my hair
down the middle, she shivered.
Or I shivered.
Hold still, she scolded me,
pinching my chin.

Through her window
I saw, for the first time
to know it, the world outside
me. What has always
refused to hold still.

Sunday morning.
A bell ringing somewhere.
Her shawl hung upon me like snow
that would soon bend the branches.
Or break them.

She unlatched the door.
By my own name, she led me
outside into cold wind that silenced
her. I held my breath.
She held on tight to my hands.

Looking up at the ruins of them,
ragged edges those dead trees
        raise against the sky, and beyond
    them the cut of a hawk's wing,
        the curve of the river
of cloud shapes, I'm likely to squander
        this morning with dreaming them
turned back to women again, having grown
        old along with these mountains

and left here to die like the rest of us.
        I'd sit for hours and watch,
if I could, how the wind through their branches
        keeps trying to make them sway,
    supple as girls again, line dancing
        over the rocky horizon of Snowbird.
        But not much of morning's left.
I should be piecing a new quilt or mending
    my husband's socks. I should be stirring

    the beans left to scorch in the pot.
        What does wind whisper
    up there of death? Or is dancing
the gist of it? As for my need to bear witness
        to all I cannot keep from dying,
the truth is I've never liked loose ends.
        Just look at my quilts: a succession
        of rings, wreaths, and whirligigs.
        Threaded since daybreak,

        my needle waits here on the table
as if to remind me how stitches too small
        to be known save by touch
    of the thread toiling under my fingers
        can fashion a way out of one death and into
another. So stand up, I tell myself.
        Shake out your stiff limbs and sway
    like your sisters up there on the ridge,
still in line for the next dancing lesson.

Living with us
while she taught at the school
down on Eagle's Eye Creek,
she would now and again
teach me words for the commonest
things. Love
and death. Bread and
water. A dead language
she called it, nobody anymore
spoke it, but deep
in its sounds burned the homefire
of words such as *vision,*
and *navigate,*
even the sweetest of
names to me, *dulcimer.*
Over and over she made me pronounce
Sicut aquila juvenescum:
Like the eagle, I shall grow up.
She could sing in that language,
and did so
the night of Old Christmas,
Epiphany she called it,
stemming from Greek,
like my own name
of Delphia. She was too smart
to stay long, said my daddy,
and sure enough she packed her bags
come the first thaw.
Announced she was going back home
to the flatlands to marry
somebody or other
and although she cried
when the buggy came,
grabbing my hand
and declaring she'd write
me a real letter someday,
we none of us ever did
hear what became of her.

This story goes way back,
the tinkers who passed through our cove
every summer would say before
singing its mournfulness over the jangle

of kitchen goods swinging
from ribbons that looked to be dyed
in the blood of some wounded
wild animal. How could a child fathom

such riddles? A woman who gives up
for God her true lover and listens
the rest of her days to the sea in her head
sounded crazy. Or cursed. God

to me always meant so much Preacher
Talk: *Here on the altar of time will the Lord*
thy God sacrifice all things most precious
to thee. How a woman in love could defy

love itself I did not understand
until years later, I lay in pinestraw,
his hands at the hooks of my bodice,
and felt such a tide round my petticoat gather

as I feared would soon drag me under.
I saw then what God Himself prophesied.
Nothing but crumbled stone where
once our cabin had stood. Next to nothing

where once on my finger a ring,
on my lips. . . . Oh, that old song was spinning
me round as I pushed him away. *Gone,*
I told him, *like all the rest soon*

you will be, so you might as well go
now. And turning my face to the wall

of air waiting, I heard what I thought
was the wind, how it croons like an ocean

up this high. I swayed on the edge of it,
ready to be swept away, having all but forgotten
the shell-horn he held to my ear while
he whispered how deep

in its coils I could hear my own blood
singing back to itself.
Like a fire, he said.
Not the sea.

carrot, it rises
each summer from weeds with no fanfare,
no story
save how it lay low beneath ice crust
or bracken,
and waited.

But call it Queen Anne's lace
and it would have taken her women all winter to make,
huddled under a small window,
guiding white thread on its journey through pins
like a labyrinth stuck into lap cushions.
Water against dirty stone of the castle froze shut

any musical passage, but sometimes
the screams of a child who had fallen through
ice caused their fingers to falter.
When wind down the chimney blew soot in their eyes,
who could tell what was primrose,
what sweet amaryllis?

By May they'd have knotted the roots
of the last weeping willow tree. Plowshares cut
into the stubble and maidens wore
daisy crowns down to the fish markets, singing
they needed no fine lace to make them look comely.
Did she never hear them, confined to her chamber

with no royal infant to suckle?
Ivory lace in her bodice stanched milk
she must let dry up. Hot cloths of old lace for milk pain
and cold cloths for fever. Her hands pushed their way
through her mourning black sleeves,
at the cuffs but a pittance of lace to console her,
else she might have kept to her bed,
never unclenched her fist for a kiss.

So much lace.
There's no end to it
strewn along crossties and fenceposts
or stitching its stubborn way through
to the edge of each backcountry road.
Call it wild
if you choose.
Or an unhappy queen's sole indulgence.
Come June
in the Blue Ridge
there's hardly a woman who hasn't
herself longed for lace
or to let fall its trappings
among yellow milkwort and lowliest meadow rue.

Hunted to death
for a five-dollar bounty,
the wolf has been gone
from these mountains

a hundred years,
save in the blood
of some yellow-eyed stray
with a fierce opposition

to choke chain
and all human boundaries.
The Cherokee knew him
as Wa'ya, the watchdog

of huntsman Kanaʻtĭ.
No mortal dared track
him for fear
of the wolf spirit's vengeance.

When Wa'ya howled
over the snow-crusted passes,
the fire in the sacred lodge
trembled. The young braves

grew restless when Wa'ya's pack
milled at the border
of broomsedge surrounding
the cornfields of Oconaluftee.

When wolves roam the stories
we tell about taming these mountains
where, strangled by kudzu, the old dens
still wait in the darkness,

we listen for echoes
of what used to challenge the drunken

brag passed around hunters' fires.
Shape notes of night itself.

Blood
on its breath,
after which followed nothing
but silence.

1

Named for the hunter
who whistled
his wolves to the chase
in those days we call
wilderness,
this very trail
might have carried
him into another
of his rowdy stories
where aʻwĭ´,
sălâ´lĭ,
tsuʻlă,
the Cherokee names
for the hunted ones, pulsed
in the shadows.
A long time it's taken us,
searching for home in these mountains,
to learn, like Kanaʻtĭ's wife,
clever Selu of the cornpatch,
that blood washed away in the river
can come back to life,
crying out its abandonment.

2

Up from the shallows
stepped Wild Boy
who said to Kanaʻtĭ's son,
I am your brother.

Then Selu understood
he had sprung from the blood
of Kanaʻtĭ's kill she'd skinned
and gutted alongside the river.

3

Trillium raise up their three-pointed stars
among branch lettuce swarming the creek banks
that local tribes still come to harvest.
My grandmother called those greens

squaw salad, said they'd be likely
to turn your mouth inside
out, leave you muttering words
you had better not swallow

else you'd surely choke
on them, foam at the mouth,
gnaw your hungry tongue clean through
with wanting to run wild again.

4

Like cairns marking some ancient God's
visitation, these mountains in early spring
promise a way home, their roots

of a million trees holding this long
climb together for me,
so that I might arrive at the top

of the ridge where a sign
pointing three ways invites
me to stop and consider which

path. Before turning
back, taking the right
or the left fork to some other name,

I must rest for a while,
catch my breath
on a hickory stump.

If an old hunter
stepped from the shadows,
wrapped tight as a wound

in his blanket of skins, what would
I have to answer
for? Stalled at his crossroads

I climbed half
of daylight to reach,
I hear blood in my ears

drum the oldest
of riddles. The one unto
death demands I

be the answer.

Over frozen weeds,
I let my shawl drag its black fringes,
hauling up spent leaves

and husks like a net
in which I've become tangled.
To wind its length all the way

round me, I cast
its warp wide as the span
of a raptor's wings.

I used to see
myself fierce as the gleam
in an unblinking eagle's eye.

Now I see only an old
woman hunched over cold
hoecake crumbs in my lap

while I take stock
of what I still know,
over which stone

my wet garments lay
and from which limb my fleece lifted
out of the dye pot dripped

indigo, rose
madder, brightest
of hickory-bark yellow.

With which bucket did
I draw up from the well's silence
water and more water?

Granny they call me.
When they think I can't hear them, hag.
The hag of Blood Mountain.

My real name?
A fiddle string snapped in the course
of a slip jig, the sound of no more left,

go home now, the fun's
over. Wind spins the leaves
round my feet like a tide

shifting. Sail away,
I used to sing, in the swim
of things. Even then

I could feel deep water
tugging my buck-and-wing
I loved to dance

on the wooden floor.
Soon it will carry
me out, past the offing

and into that yonder
sea. Blue nothing
I call it. Calling me.

Wherever I walk in this house
I hear water. Or time.
Which is water, the same

Tuckasegee that runs past my window.
What matter that some days I weary
of it like the songs I hum
over and over again in the kitchen
pretending I cannot hear water departing
though I so plainly hear it
if only from habit? A sequence

of bones rots beneath where I walk
on the trail that unwinds down the hill
to our yard where the leaves also rot.

Every morning I braid what is left
of my hair so that I may unbraid it to braid
it again. So we harvest our gardens

that winter will lay waste.
We mend seams that pull apart
slowly and scrub sweat from what
we have sewn. With the same hands
we knead bread and gather the crumbs
as they fall, put away
what we take out and take stock
of what we have left. It is all the same

work. It has always been
done, this undoing,
ongoing, no matter who
paces the rooms of the houses
alongside the banks,
whether praising
or cursing whatever is living
or dying within them. Until

it runs out like the river,
our time is the music
the water makes, leaving
who's left of us listening.

Down to the cow stall
again she goes
that she might sit knee
to knee with an old woman

done now for good
with her milking and ready
to sing forth her final
instructions: "Oh

soon will her lily hand
threading the heddles be gone
and so deep in the muddy strand
draggled her silk gowden

fringes." Each woman's voice
echoes the other as verse after verse
draws the sly Gypsy Dave ever
closer to her empty pockets,

the buttons he'll unbutton
down to the hem of her coat.
With her eyes closed, she's singing
him back through the centuries

until she's caught
in a last kiss so wild she can't
stop him, his black-stubbled
mouth on her throat.

N O T E S

Three of these poems are transplanted from early Celtic poems as found in *Sources and Analogs of Old English Poetry II,* trans. Daniel G. Calder *et al.* (Cambridge, England, and Totowa, N.J., 1983).

"Snow Breath" (p. 12) was written in response to a Welsh poem, "Eiry Mynydd," from *The Red Book of Hergest,* composed between the ninth and twelfth centuries.

"Sea Change" (p. 39) is an Appalachian response to the ninth-century Irish poem "Cen áinius" (Líadan Speaks of Cuirithir).

"Backwater" (p. 48) is an Appalachian version of the ninth-century Irish poem "Caillech Bérri" (The Hag of Beare).

Page 25: Phacelia is a wildflower that blooms in April whose blossoms from a distance are said to look like beds of snow.

Page 45: Some of the material in "Kanati" was taken from James Mooney's *Myths of the Cherokee,* reproduced in 1982 by Charles and Randy Elder—Booksellers/Publishers, Nashville, in collaboration with Cherokee Heritage Books, Cherokee, N.C.

Page 52: "Síle" is the Gaelic spelling of Sheila. This poem is for Sheila Kay Adams, seventh-generation ballad singer from Madison County, North Carolina, and in memory of her Granny Dell, Mrs. Dellie Norton, who taught her, "knee to knee," the old ballads brought from Scotland and Ireland.